10.49

DISASTER!

VOLCANOES

By Dennis Brindell Fradin

Consultant:
Alfred T. Anderson, Jr., Ph. D.
Associate Professor of Geology
University of Chicago

CHILDRENS PRESS, CHICAGO

Harry R. Truman (above) sits on the steps of his St. Helens Lodge
on Spirit Lake. Even though the area had been evacuated and roadblocks
had been set up to keep people out of the Red Zone (below), Mr. Truman
refused to leave the area where he had lived for more than fifty years.

1/MOUNT ST. HELENS - 1980

In March of 1980 many people heard about Mount St. Helens for the first time. Scientists had detected small earthquakes near the Washington volcano. It might be getting ready to erupt, they warned. On March 27 an explosion blew a 200-foot hole out of the mountain. The next day Mount St. Helens sent steam, gas, and ash four miles into the sky.

These were the first volcanic eruptions from Mount St. Helens since 1857, more than a hundred years earlier. Except for volcanoes in Alaska and Hawaii, Mount St. Helens was the first volcano to erupt *anywhere* in the United States since California's Lassen Peak erupted in 1917. But scientists feared that these March eruptions were only the beginning. They warned that the volcano's main eruption might be yet to come.

Anyone in the path of a big eruption would be in great danger from ash, heat, and deadly gas. Mount St. Helens— with its lovely forests and lakes—was a popular vacation playground. Climbers, campers, and fishermen enjoyed the mountain and its surrounding area. A big eruption could kill hundreds of people.

As a precaution, federal and Washington state officials marked off an area around Mount St. Helens. This area was called the *Red Zone*. If the mountain should erupt, destruction in the Red Zone was expected to be the most severe. Roadblocks were set up to keep people out of the Red Zone. But not everyone stayed out. Some campers and loggers went in on old logging roads. And several people who lived in the area refused to leave their homes. Harry R. Truman, owner of the St. Helens Lodge, had lived on the

*This scenic view of Mount St. Helens and
Spirit Lake was taken in the summer of 1959.*

northeast side of the mountain for more than fifty years. "I am part of that mountain, the mountain is part of me," the eighty-four-year-old man said. He refused to leave his home.

Despite the danger, scientists moved in close to the peak so they could observe the volcano. The United States Geological Survey (USGS) sent in more than two dozen scientists. Using various instruments, they monitored Mount St. Helens in an effort to determine when it might erupt. David Johnston, a thirty-year-old USGS scientist, was assigned a post six miles north of the peak. Scientists expected Mount St. Helens to erupt straight up into the air. Six miles seemed a safe enough distance.

The great eruption that scientists had expected came on the morning of Sunday, May 18, 1980. It started with earthquakes and landslides at 8:27 and 8:31 in the morning. The landslides helped release the gas that was trapped inside the volcano. At 8:32 A.M. ash, smoke, and gases erupted from the throat of the mountain. But instead of going straight up into the sky, the volcanic blast headed sideways, toward the north.

Three days after the first Mount St. Helens explosion on March 27, 1980, the mountain was still erupting steam (above left). Then, on May 18, a huge blast tore away the whole top of the mountain (above right).

"Vancouver! Vancouver! This is it!" David Johnston reported by radio to the local USGS headquarters in Vancouver, Washington. Those were Johnston's last words. Very soon after he spoke them, he was crushed under tons of rocks. Harry R. Truman met the same death at his St. Helens Lodge.

The force of the blast was as great as the largest hydrogen bomb ever exploded. Several miles from the eruption, logging trucks and bulldozers were sent flying through the air like toys. To the north, trees up to twenty miles away from the peak were torn up and hurled about as if they were sticks.

People close to the mountain's north side saw the ash and gas cloud approach them at two hundred miles per hour. One man climbed a tree. Others went into their cars. But there was no place to hide. The volcano had many ways to kill. Ash, deadly gas, flying rocks, and heat from the eruption killed about sixty-five people. Some of these victims were eighteen miles away at the time of the eruption. Millions of deer, elk, birds, and other animals also were killed.

During the weeks before the major eruption, geologists (below) monitored Mount St. Helens in an effort to determine when the explosion might occur.

Ash from the Mount St. Helens eruption turned the Sunday afternoon sky in Yakima, Washington as black as night (above). Anyone on the streets that day had to wear a face mask to avoid breathing the drifting ash.

Ash from the eruption drifted high into the sky. Then it began to spread across the country. The thick ash and smoke blocked out the light of the sun over a wide area. At Yakima—85 miles east of Mount St. Helens—the sky turned as black as night. At Walla Walla—190 miles east—the morning sky grew so dark that street lights automatically went on. During the next few days, drifting ash could be seen in many places across the United States. Ash settled on crops in Washington's Yakima Valley and in fields as far away as Oregon and Idaho. Wheat, apples, hay, and other crops were damaged by the ashfall.

Back at Mount St. Helens, the eruption had caused a mudflow down the west side of the mountain. This mudflow caused floods of the Toutle, Cowlitz, and Columbia rivers. Floodwaters washed away bridges and houses. Some houses that weren't washed away were buried up to their rooftops in mud. Trout and salmon died by the millions in the mud-filled rivers.

When the volcano finally quieted, people saw a vastly

This two-story home is engulfed in mud from the flooded Toutle River.

The May 18 eruption ripped away 1,300 feet from the top of Mount St. Helens. Spirit Lake had become a mess of logs and muck.

altered landscape. On May 17, Mount St. Helens had been the fifth-tallest peak in Washington. Now, on May 18, it was only the thirteenth-tallest peak. The eruption had ripped away 1,300 feet of mountaintop. The once-lovely lakes in the area were a mess of logs and muck. With forests flattened, wildlife was nowhere to be seen.

But Mount St. Helens will not always be barren, scientists say. In time, rain and water from snow will cleanse the lakes and rivers. The wind will blow in seeds that will grow into new plants. The plant materials will mix with the volcanic ash to create new soil. Trees will take root in the ground and animals will return to live in the new forests.

But unlike the process of destruction that took only minutes, this process of renewal will take many years.

Top: This picture of Spirit Lake was taken only a few minutes before the great eruption on the morning of May 18, 1980. Though it will take years for new forests to replace the thousands of acres devastated by the Mount St. Helens blast (above), within four months there was new growth of fireweed on the periphery of the blast zone (left).

Mount St. Helens, still active on July 22, 1980, emits a plume of
steam and ash (above). Mount Hood, visible in the background, has been
subject to recent earthquakes, which may mean that this previously
inactive volcano will become active in the near future.
This aerial view of Mount St. Helens (below), taken on November 7, 1980,
shows the section of the mountain that was torn away by the blast of
May 18. A growing lava dome can be seen in the center of the crater.

2/SURVIVORS - MOUNT ST. HELENS, 1980

We are waiting death at any moment. A mountain has burst near here. We are covered with ashes, in some places 10 feet and 6 feet deep. All this began June 6. Night and day we light lanterns. We cannot see the daylight. We have no water, the rivers are just ashes mixed with water. Here are darkness and hell, thunder and noise. I do not know whether it is day or night. The earth is trembling, it lightens every minute. It is terrible. We are praying.

Letter written by Ivan
Orloff to his wife during
the 1912 eruption of
Mount Katmai in Alaska

I can hear the mountain rumbling behind me, I feel the ash in my eyes. Oh dear God, this is hell. . . it's a black hell, totally pitch black . . . . Dear God, help me breathe. I can't see a thing.

Tape recording made during
the 1980 Mount St. Helens
eruption by television photographer
David Crockett, who survived
the blast

Occasionally, we read or hear such on-the-spot descriptions of erupting volcanoes. More often, we must rely on survivors to remember what a blast was like. About two hundred people managed to live through the Mount St. Helens eruption. Following are the stories of several survivors, and also the story of a rescuer.

13

Dorothy and Keith Stoffel, Survivors

When Mount St. Helens erupted, Dorthy and Keith Stoffel were in one of the worst possible places—inside an airplane 1,000 feet above the mountain.

Their adventure began early on the morning of May 18, when they climbed into a single-engine airplane at the Yakima, Washington airport. The Stoffels are both geologists. The USGS had given them permission to fly over the Red Zone to study and photograph the volcano. There were no signs of an impending eruption, so it didn't appear to be a dangerous flight.

"We had chartered the airplane flight to celebrate my thirty-first birthday," Dorothy Stoffel said later, as she and her husband related the experience. "We had never seen an active volcano before," said Keith Stoffel. "It was the chance of a lifetime—a chance that comes only once in *many* lifetimes."

The two geologists were excited as the plane neared Mount St. Helens. They arrived over the restricted zone at 7:50 A.M. Their pilot, Bruce Judson, made three passes around Mount St. Helens and two right over the crater. "The crater was absolutely serene," Dorothy Stoffel recalled. "In fact, there was so little activity that I thought the volcano was going into dormancy."

The Stoffels asked Judson to make one more pass to the east, over the crater, before returning to Yakima. As they were directly over the crater, Dorothy Stoffel noticed some steam coming from it. A lot happened in the next seconds.

At 8:31, they witnessed an earthquake. "It looked as if a knife were slicing the volcano in half," Dorothy Stoffel said. "The glaciers on the northern half of Mount St. Helens

At 8:32 A.M., the moment of the blast, Keith and Dorothy Stoffel took this picture from the single-engine airplane in which they were flying to observe Mount St. Helens on the morning of May 18, 1980.

cascaded into the mountain. Then we could see the northern half of the mountain falling and sliding away beneath us."

At 8:32, the Stoffels witnessed a two-part eruption. "The first, smaller blast came at the fracture where the mountain had broken apart," said Keith Stoffel. "Only ten seconds before, our airplane had been in the direct path of that first blast."

Dorothy and Keith Stoffel didn't have time to think about this first close call. Within seconds, a huge blast exploded sideways from the volcano. The blast cloud headed right toward the small airplane.

Geologists Keith and Dorothy Stoffel

For precious seconds, the Stoffels and their pilot stared in disbelief as the cloud approached. "It was overwhelming—I was in shock," Dorothy Stoffel remembered. But Keith Stoffel yelled to the pilot, "Get out of here!" He told him to head south, in the opposite direction from the blast.

To gain speed, Bruce Judson dived the airplane. "We were flying over two hundred miles per hour, but the blast fanned out so quickly it appeared to overhaul us before we could get clear," Dorothy Stoffel remembered.

They'll never know how close the cloud came to the airplane. The important fact was that they did get clear of the cloud. When they were safely away, they looked back at the mountain. "We saw a big blast column rising 60,000 feet into the sky," Dorothy Stoffel said. "As this column was developing, there was the most incredible lightning I have ever seen. I could see the whole throat of the volcano lit up by the lightning. It was like looking down into the throat of hell."

Bruce Judson landed in Portland, Oregon. Weeks after returning to their home in Spokane, Washington, the Stoffels

16

were still shaken. But they had done more than survive a dangerous experience. They brought back some important geological observations and photographs. Many geologists had expected the volcano to give some warning in the hours before a big eruption. The Stoffels' photos show that the mountain was quiet just minutes before the eruption. The Stoffels also observed that earthquakes triggered the eruptions, and that there were at least two separate parts to the eruption.

Their sense of hearing provided one of their most interesting observations. "Never through the whole experience did we hear anything," Dorothy Stoffel said. "It was like watching a silent movie." Other observers in the blast area also reported that they heard no noise. Yet people hundreds of miles away heard the sound of the blast. Scientists disagree about the reasons for this.

In summing up her feelings about the experience, Dorothy Stoffel said: "Geologically, this eruption wasn't that big compared to some others in the past. But it was big in terms of what modern people have experienced. I myself have studied volcanoes for years, but even to me volcanic eruptions always seemed just like stories or very old history. This event hit home that these things aren't just stories, they aren't just history. They really do happen."

Sue Ruff and Bruce Nelson, Survivors

Months after the eruption, Sue Ruff still was having nightmares about her ordeal.

In the spring of 1980 Sue Ruff was a twenty-one-year-old college student who lived in Kelso, Washington. Sue's twenty-two-year-old fiancé, Bruce Nelson, worked in a bakery in Kelso. Both young people loved to camp and backpack.

On Friday, May 16, Sue and Bruce drove in on a logging road and set up camp on the Green River about fourteen miles north of Mount St. Helens. "We picked the area because it was a beautiful place to hike, swim, and fish," Sue recalled.

"We were quite a way below the roadblock and no one tried to stop us," said Bruce. "Fourteen miles seemed like a safe distance from the volcano."

By Saturday, four friends had joined Sue and Bruce. The six young people hiked, fished, and explored. They even took pictures of each other standing next to some huge two-hundred-year-old trees. They had no idea that on Sunday morning those trees would be falling all around them.

"On Sunday morning our friend Terry Crall noticed a strange-looking cloud in the distance and he said it must be a forest fire. We looked at it and told each other it wasn't any forest fire," Sue recalled. "Terry went into his tent to wake up his girl friend, Karen Varner."

"Sue and I were watching the cloud and walking backward in amazement," continued Bruce. "The cloud reached out closer and closer to us like it had arms. Before it got to us there was one of the strongest windstorms I've ever felt in my life. It blew our fire flat onto the ground. Then we heard the noise of trees coming down."

Fortunately, Sue and Bruce fell into a hole that had been created when a huge tree was uprooted. Trees fell on top of the hole, so that Sue and Bruce were in a kind of underground cave.

About a minute after the hurricanelike wind, Bruce started

The enormous explosion of Mount St. Helens (left) created terrific windstorms that blew down millions of trees, including those that fell on Sue Ruff and Bruce Nelson's camping area.

to climb out of the hole. He was part-way out when the heat wave came. The intense heat burned the hair on his arms and legs and forced him back down beneath the fallen trees. The trees protected Bruce and Sue from the heat. But it didn't protect them from the ash and gas. Choking and gasping for air, Sue and Bruce knew they had to escape from the area. But they couldn't see. The ash had blocked out the light from the sun.

"As we left the valley we couldn't even see the hands in front of our faces," said Sue. "We wrapped our shirts around our heads to filter out the ash and help us breathe. We were getting hit by wood, rock, and ice thrown off the mountain. There was also lightning right over our heads. The volcano had created its own electrical storm."

Sue and Bruce crawled under a log and waited two hours until things quieted. Then—though the ash was still so hot

that it was melting their boots—Bruce and Sue made their
way back to camp. They wanted to find their friends. They
called for Terry and Karen. There was no answer, and there
was no sign of the tent. Sue and Bruce did find their other two
friends—Brian Thomas and Dan Balch. Brian could barely
move because a falling tree had dislocated his hip. Dan had
terrible burns on his arms and legs from the heat blast.

Off in the distance, earthquakes could be heard. "We
didn't know if the volcano would erupt again," said Sue. "We
thought it best that the ones who were unhurt go for help."
They found an abandoned miner's shack and left Brian there.
Dan was left by the Green River so that he could soak his
arms and feet in the water. Sue and Bruce then left the valley
to find help.

Their plan was to make it to Camp Baker, a logging camp.
On the way there, Sue and Bruce met logger Grant
Christensen. Before ash overcame his truck, Christensen had
managed to talk by CB radio to some people in the area. They
had told Christensen that they would meet him if he headed
north. Sue and Bruce decided to head north with Christensen.
This was a stroke of luck for them. Had they approached
Camp Baker, Sue and Bruce might have encountered the
mudflow that struck the logging camp.

Grant Christensen's friends never did find them. At about
7:30 P.M. Sue, Bruce, and Grant reached the "2400" road.
Suddenly a helicopter appeared above them.

"We started hitting the ground with our shirts to kick up
the ash," said Sue. "We were afraid the pilot wouldn't see
us." The pilot spotted them and made a dangerous landing.
Bruce, Sue, and Grant were saved. But as they headed back
toward their camp in the helicopter, Bruce and Sue were
extremely worried about their friends.

Mike Cairns, Rescuer

The helicopter pilot who rescued Sue Ruff and Bruce
Nelson was thirty-three-year-old Mike Cairns, a Vietnam War
veteran and a captain in the Washington National Guard.

As soon as the volcano erupted, a number of federal, state,
and county rescue organizations went into action. The
Washington National Guard was not the only rescue group
involved. Others were the United States Forest Service, Air
Force reserve units, the United States Army, the sheriffs'
offices of several Washington counties, and various volunteer
rescue units in the state. Their rescue efforts were
coordinated by the Washington State Department of
Emergency Services.

When the eruption occurred, Mike Cairns was with his
helicopter unit in Yakima, Washington. The unit had just
begun their yearly two weeks of "active drill." The purpose
of the drilling was to get them ready for combat if they were
ever needed in a war. But the Washington National Guard
also had the job of helping in flood relief and rescue
operations in the state. In the previous weeks, Cairns'
helicopter unit had readied itself for rescue missions in
case Mount St. Helens erupted.

"At about nine in the morning I was sitting at a meeting in
Yakima when we saw what we thought was a thunderstorm
coming from the west," Cairns recalled. "There was lightning
in the cloud and lots of turbulence. The phone rang and we
found out that the volcano had erupted.

"We had about twenty helicopters on the ground ready to
go. Twelve made it off the ground. The others couldn't get
out in time because they were already socked in by ash.

"Ash was falling all over the windshield as we took off, and then it turned pitch black. For about fifteen minutes we flew by instruments in total darkness.''

The area had been divided into various search sectors. Cairns and another helicopter pilot were assigned to search the south fork of the Toutle River. Near the beginning of their search, Cairns and his two-man crew spotted a pickup truck that contained three people. But when he hovered down near the pickup, Cairns saw that the people were dead.

"Then we spotted some tracks and followed them for about three miles," Cairns said. "We saw three people waving their shirts and kicking up ash."

Cairns prepared to land on a bend in the road. But within twenty feet of the ground, the chopper kicked up so much ash that Cairns had no visibility. Slowly and carefully, he managed to land the helicopter. After waiting for the ash to settle, he got out of the aircraft and went up a hill toward the three people.

"I'm sure glad I found you," he said, giving them a hug.

"Not half as glad as I am!" Sue Ruff said.

"Can you direct us to any other survivors?" asked Cairns.

Sue and Bruce told him about Brian, Dan, Terry, and Karen.

They flew about ten miles back to the Green River and spotted Brian Thomas. He had dragged himself from the cabin and was hiding under a bridge in case the volcano erupted again. By this time, Cairns' helicopter was low on fuel. He called in another chopper to rescue Brian Thomas. Dan Balch, too, had been spotted at the river and was rescued by a National Guard chopper. But there was no sign of Terry and Karen.

At this point, Cairns flew Sue, Bruce, and Grant Christensen to the Longview-Kelso Airport. Except for some scratches and burns, there was nothing physically wrong with Sue and Bruce. They went home.

Mike Cairns, however, continued his rescue efforts for the next three weeks. Although dozens of people were rescued by the National Guard, Mike Cairns found no more living people. His job became one of retrieving bodies.

"Everyone I saw within twelve miles of the eruption had been killed," he said. "What I saw at that mountain was unreal. I saw a new motor home with its whole front end melted by the heat. Six miles from the blast I saw a construction Caterpillar weighing about 120,000 pounds blown upside down with parts of it melted."

While Mike Cairns was retrieving bodies, Sue and Bruce wondered about their friends Terry Crall and Karen Varner. There was a slim chance that somehow they had survived. The Thursday after the great eruption, Mike Cairns took Bruce and two Cowlitz County sheriff's deputies into the area where the young people's camp had been. They landed and walked toward the camping area.

They found the tent buried under some trees. Using chain saws, they cut the trees apart. They found the bodies of Terry and Karen with their arms around each other. Both had been killed instantly by a falling tree.

Mike Cairns and Bruce Nelson then made what was probably the last rescue of a living creature after the eruption. Terry and Karen had brought a pet dog and her puppies with them on the camping trip. The mother dog was pinned under some logs. Her puppies were standing near her and barking. Using the saws, Mike Cairns and Bruce Nelson cut the mother dog free. They took the dog and her puppies back with the bodies of Terry and Karen. Bruce and Sue still have those dogs today.

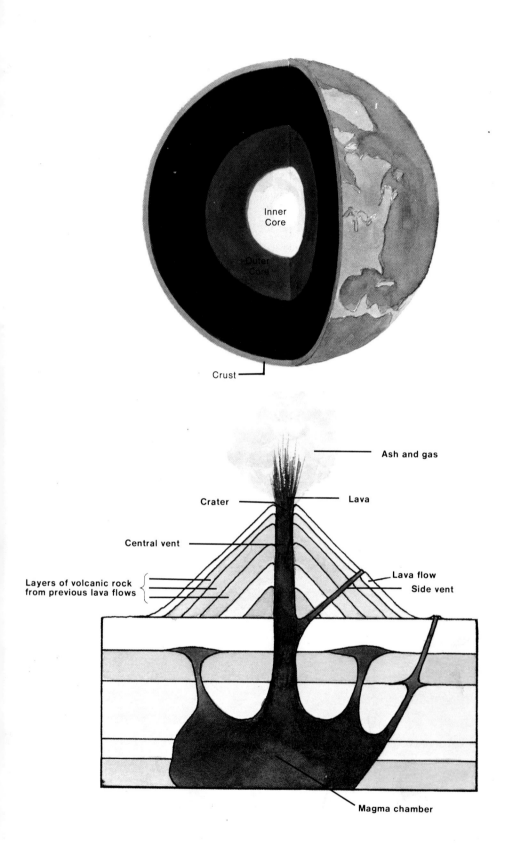

Inner
Core

Outer
Core

Crust

Ash and gas

Crater

Lava

Central vent

Layers of volcanic rock
from previous lava flows

Lava flow

Side vent

Magma chamber

3/HOW VOLCANOES WORK AND HOW SCIENTISTS STUDY THEM

The eruption of Mount St. Helens could have claimed hundreds of lives. But because scientists suspected that a big eruption was coming, people were kept out of the area. The scientists didn't use a crystal ball to predict the eruption. They used their knowledge about how volcanoes work.

The special study of volcanoes is called *volcanology*. The scientists who study volcanoes are called *volcanologists*. *Geologists*—scientists who study the earth—also include volcanoes in their field of interest.

These scientists can't go deep inside the earth where volcanoes have their beginnings. So they must be detectives. They look at such "clues" as rocks and other materials that are thrown out of volcanoes. Based on studies of these clues, scientists now agree on many aspects of how volcanoes work.

To understand volcanoes, the scientists tell us, we should first know about the structure of our planet Earth. The earth is made up of several layers. The outside layer is called the *crust*. It is made of rock. Under the continents, the crust is as much as twenty miles thick. Under the oceans, it is about three to five miles thick.

Beneath the crust, there is a huge region of our planet called the *mantle*. It is made of very hot rock. The earth's mantle extends beneath us to a depth of about 1,800 miles. The mantle is almost completely solid. But about 75 miles beneath the surface of the earth, the temperature is about 2,500° F. and the pressure is 40,000 times greater than at the earth's surface. There, part of the rock melts. This melted rock is called *magma*.

Some magma stays inside the earth. But other magma rises

toward the earth's surface. This happens because the magma is lighter than the rocks around it.

Higher and higher toward the surface the magma rises. It may form a *magma chamber* just a few miles beneath the ground. This chamber is like a huge underground blister of magma.

Gas bubbles in the magma build up pressure that helps force it to higher and higher levels. Sometimes the pressure becomes so great that the magma makes a crack all the way up to the earth's surface. Or—as in the case of Mount St. Helens and other volcanoes that have erupted—the magma explodes through a crack formed by a previous eruption. In either case, the magma bursts right out of the ground.

The crack through which the magma comes is called a *volcano*. After an eruption, material from under the ground piles up around the crack and forms a mountain. This mountain also is called a *volcano*.

When the magma flows out of the ground it is called *lava*. Lava is very hot—sometimes over 2,000° F. Some lava glows brightly, like fire. But most is covered with a dark coating of hot rock. Although lava can set trees and buildings on fire, it is the least dangerous of all material erupted from volcanoes. People are rarely hurt by lava. They can see and hear it coming and get out of the way.

The *volcanic gas* released by the lava is far deadlier than the lava itself. Poisonous gas has killed more people than lava has. The gas lacks oxygen, and we cannot breathe it.

Deadly, too, are the hot rock fragments that explode from the volcano. The smallest pieces—no bigger than dust—are called *volcanic dust*. Volcanic dust is so light that it is often blown high into the atmosphere. *Volcanic ash* is a little larger than volcanic dust, but each piece is still less than a fifth of an

This night view shows glowing lava erupting from Parícutin Volcano in 1943.

inch in diameter. Volcanic ash from the Mount St. Helens blast choked many people to death. The biggest rocks blown out of a volcano are called *volcanic bombs.* Some volcanic bombs weigh many tons. People who have survived eruptions in which there have been volcanic bombs have compared it to playing a deadly game of dodgeball.

Volcanic eruptions vary greatly in size and violence. In the mildest eruptions, there is just a lava flow. Other eruptions produce mainly hot ash and gas. In the most violent eruptions, the gas trapped inside the magma builds up great pressure. The result is an explosion producing great glowing clouds of dust and ash.

Different kinds of eruptions create different kinds of volcanic mountains. Volcanologists have classified volcanic mountains into three types.

The first kind is called the *shield volcano*. This is a mountain formed almost completely by lava flows. It has gentle slopes and may have craters on the top. Mauna Loa in Hawaii is a shield volcano.

The second type of volcano is the *cinder cone*. This is a cone-shaped mountain built from eruptions of cinders, ash, and other rock fragments. Paricutin in Mexico and Stromboli in the Mediterranean Sea are two examples of cinder cones.

The *composite volcano* is the third type. A composite volcano is made up of both lava and rock fragments. Composite volcanoes are shaped something like an upside-down V. Mount Vesuvius in Italy, Mount Fuji in Japan, and Mount St. Helens are three examples of composite volcanoes.

A hundred years or more may pass between eruptions of a volcano. That may sound like a long time. But in the life of our planet Earth, a hundred years is a very short time. Generations of human beings can live near a volcano and never see it stir. Then it may suddenly roar to life.

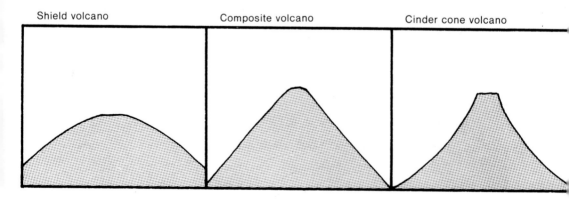

Shield volcano   Composite volcano   Cinder cone volcano

Japan's Mount Fuji (left) is a composite volcano.

Scientists have terms to classify just how "alive" each volcano is. Volcanoes that have erupted within the past few years—or have shown signs of erupting—are called *active*. Active volcanoes might very well erupt in the not-too-distant future.

Volcanoes that have been quiet in recent years but have erupted within the past several centuries are called *dormant*, meaning sleeping. They could still roar back to life at some future time. Before Mount St. Helens began to stir in 1980, it was considered dormant.

Volcanoes that have not erupted since history began are said to be *extinct*, meaning dead. But because we can't see inside the earth, it is impossible to be sure that a volcano is totally extinct. Lassen Peak in California was once considered extinct. But it erupted in 1914 and continued to erupt for three years. Arenal Volcano in Costa Rica had been called extinct, too—until it erupted in 1968.

Still, it is the active volcanoes that are most likely to erupt and kill people. So it is the active volcanoes that scientists

In the weeks before Mount St. Helens exploded (above), scientists used many methods to study the mountain and try to predict when it would erupt.

watch most closely. There are even observatories on the sides of some volcanic mountains so that scientists can watch for signs of eruption.

How Scientists Study Volcanoes and Predict Eruptions

Scientists use what they know about how volcanoes work to predict when one might erupt. They have a number of instruments to help them.

You will remember that before a volcano erupts, magma moves up from beneath the ground. As the magma rises, earthquakes may occur. Scientists use an instrument called a *seismograph* to detect such earthquakes. When shocks in a volcanic mountain are detected, the scientists become alert to the possibility of eruption.

As a mountain gets ready to explode, its sides often swell. This makes the mountain's slopes a tiny bit steeper. An instrument called a *tiltmeter* measures this swelling. The tiltmeter is very sensitive. It can detect even a very small amount of swelling.

Scientists use *gas detectors* to check whether any unusual gas is beginning to escape from underground. The *thermometer* is an important instrument, too. Hot magma going upward heats the rock around it. So an increase in temperature is another clue that a volcano soon may erupt.

The human eye also can be a valuable tool. If large cracks begin to develop around a volcano, scientists know that the magma may be pushing its way up through the ground.

There is a way to predict an eruption even if a volcano shows no signs of stirring. Some volcanoes erupt at fairly regular intervals—every fifty or a hundred years or so. First, scientists determine the dates of previous eruptions. They can do this even if no one was there to record old eruptions. The scientists figure out the dates by studying rocks thrown out by ancient blasts.

Scientists used many of these methods to study Mount St. Helens before its May, 1980 eruption.

In the 1970s, USGS scientists Dwight Crandell and Donal Mullineaux studied the ash and mudflow deposits from previous Mount St. Helens eruptions. Using the dates of previous eruptions, they predicted that Mount St. Helens would erupt sometime before the year 2000.

The USGS sent in scientists to study the volcano. The scientists used tiltmeters to monitor the bulge in the mountain's side. They measured the temperature around the volcano and in nearby streams. David Johnston, the volcanologist who later was killed, even went down into the volcano's crater to see if volcanic gas was escaping.

These measurements showed that a great amount of activity was taking place under Mount St. Helens. This activity meant that a big eruption was a good possibility. The area was evacuated and many lives were saved.

Mount St. Helens erupted several more times after May 18, 1980, and it may continue to erupt in the future. For many years, scientists will watch Mount St. Helens for signs of another big eruption. Mount St. Helens is in the Cascade Range. USGS scientists are observing other volcanoes in the Cascade Range so that people can be cleared from the area if one of the volcanoes seems ready to erupt.

Volcanology is a very young science. Probably we will never be able to stop a volcano from erupting. But by learning more about volcanoes, scientists hope to reduce the loss of life from future eruptions.

4/MOUNT VESUVIUS-79 A.D.

Ancient people had little or no scientific knowledge about volcanoes. To many ancient people, the eruption of a volcano meant that their gods were angry.

The people of the Hawaiian Islands believed that the volcano goddess Pele caused eruptions. To keep Pele happy, the Hawaiians threw pigs—one of her favorite foods—into volcano craters. In Hawaii, the volcanic lava is so liquid that it sometimes sprays into separate drops, which then harden. The Hawaiians called the teardrop-shaped lava "Pele's tears." Lava that was spun like cotton candy as it hardened was called "Pele's hair."

The Romans—people of ancient Italy—believed that volcanoes were caused by a god named Vulcan. The word *volcano* comes from the name *Vulcan*. Vulcan was the god of fire and metalwork. He was said to do his metalwork deep under the ground. A mountain named Vulcano was his main workshop, but he had others. When a volcano in Italy smoked, the people said that Vulcan was at work making armor and weapons. But when there was a big eruption, the people said that the god of fire and metalwork was angry about something. On a day more than nineteen hundred years ago, the Roman people had reason to believe that Vulcan was *very* angry.

In the year 79 A.D. the people of Pompeii, Italy were enjoying a fine summer. Their lovely town stood at the foot of an old volcano called Mount Vesuvius. The volcano hadn't erupted for hundreds of years. Farmers were growing grapes as usual on the slopes of Mount Vesuvius. Large houses called *villas* also stood on the sides of the mountain.

In the pleasant summer of 79 A.D. the people of Pompeii, Italy had no idea that there would be a devastating eruption of Mount Vesuvius (above).

During the previous few years there had been earthquakes in the area. One in the year 63 A.D. had toppled statues and destroyed buildings. From that year until the year 79, earthquakes had damaged Pompeii. The people did not know that earthquakes often occur before an eruption. Nor did they realize at first that the "cloud" that appeared over the mountain on August 24 was ash and gas coming from the mountain.

Soon the ground shook violently as the volcano belched out ash and gas. Here and there the hot ash set fire to the countryside. Soon the ash blocked out the sun. It was so thick that Pompeii and neighboring towns were in total darkness. Many people escaped.

Those who stayed died. Some were choked to death by the volcanic gas. Others were burned and smothered by the ash.

By the time the volcano was quiet, Pompeii and the nearby town of Stabiae lay buried under volcanic ash. Another town, Herculaneum, lay buried under a mudflow that had been set off by the volcano. In all, as many as 18,000 people may have been killed by this great eruption of Mount Vesuvius.

How do we know so much about an eruption that occurred more than nineteen centuries ago? One description was provided by a man of the time named Pliny the Younger. In a letter, Pliny the Younger described how he and his mother escaped through the darkness from a town near Pompeii. He told of hearing parents call for their children in the darkness.

Pompeii lay forgotten for many centuries. But it was there—beneath twenty-three feet of ash, dust, and stone.

In 1595, some men who were building a tunnel accidentally dug up part of Pompeii. They found some statues, vases, and coins. They even uncovered remains of old buildings. In the next couple of hundred years, people began to dig pits on the site of Pompeii. They took away jewelry and vases.

The ash, dust, and rock that rained down on Pompeii from Mount Vesuvius in 79 A.D. *(below) completely buried the city.*

This fresco uncovered from the ancient city of Pompeii in 1954 adorned the wall of a tavern called the Phoenix.

Then in 1748, a farmer who was digging in a field found an underground wall. After that, Italian officials sent people to dig some more. Soon they realized that they were uncovering the ancient city of Pompeii. Little by little, workers removed the ash that covered Pompeii. The digging continues today.

You can visit the parts of Pompeii that have been uncovered. You can see buildings where the people of Pompeii lived more than 1,900 years ago. You can walk on the streets that the Pompeiians walked on, and visit the stores where they shopped. Look down at the street and you can see ruts made by chariot wheels. Look at the walls and you can see the names of some men who were running for public office so long ago. You can visit the amphitheater where sports events were held, theaters where plays and music were performed, and the forum where politicians gave speeches.

Amazingly, the remains of about two thousand people also have been found in the city. Skeletons were found in some

These plaster of Paris statues were made from perfect molds of Pompeiians who were victims of the Mount Vesuvius eruption.

houses. Those people must have stayed in their homes during the eruption. They were overcome by poisonous fumes or buried by the hot ash that caved in their roofs. Some skeletons were found holding bags of jewels or coins. Those people may have died because they wasted time to gather their valuables.

Some who went outside did not get very far. They were killed by fumes, ash, or falling rocks. Their bodies were then covered by a hard layer of ash. Over the years, the bodies disintegrated beneath the ash. But the ash had formed perfect molds of their bodies. Scientists poured plaster of Paris into the molds. The scientists were able to produce statues that showed exactly what the people looked like.

The uncovering of Pompeii has helped make Mount Vesuvius the most famous volcano in the world. Mount Vesuvius has erupted several times since 79 A.D. In the year 1631, a great eruption killed as many as 18,000 people and destroyed nearby villages. In 1906, people in the city of Naples, seven miles from Mount Vesuvius, were evacuated before a great eruption blew the top right off the cone.

A more recent eruption of Mount Vesuvius occurred in 1944, during World War II. A huge eruption produced large amounts of lava, ash, and gas. Mount Vesuvius is still very much alive. But now there is a volcano observatory on the side of the mountain. People will be evacuated when the mountain shows signs of awakening.

A huge 1944 eruption of Mount Vesuvius (below) produced large amounts of lava, gas, and ash.

5/OTHER WELL-KNOWN VOLCANOES

The eruptions of Mount Vesuvius in the year 79 and Mount St. Helens in 1980 are just two well-known volcanic blasts. There have been many other famous and interesting ones.

Krakatoa -The Blast Heard Three Thousand Miles Away

Long before there was an island called Krakatoa, there was a volcano deep below the waters of the Sunda Strait. As this volcano erupted, rock and other material piled higher and higher on the sea floor. Eventually, this mountain grew so high that it poked its head above the water. This was the island called Krakatoa. The volcano that had created the island also was called Krakatoa.

Krakatoa erupted during the 1600s, but then lay quiet for two hundred years. In the late 1870s, people on nearby islands heard and felt earthquakes from Krakatoa. The volcano was coming to life.

On May 20, 1883, three fishermen were in a boat near Krakatoa. They spotted a white cloud hanging over the volcanic peak. The cloud darkened. Suddenly there was an explosion. Rocks landed all around the fishermen's boat. The peak of the volcano had been blown off by this eruption.

Krakatoa continued to have small eruptions until August. That month, two new volcanic cracks opened on the island. Lava burst out of these cracks. Seawater rushed in. Inside the volcano, the seawater was heated into steam. There wasn't enough room inside the volcano for the expanding steam. On August 27, 1883, the expanding steam caused one of the greatest volcanic eruptions in recorded history. Most of the island of Krakatoa was blown off the face of the earth.

The sound waves from the explosion broke windows two hundred miles away. People in Australia, two thousand miles away, were awakened from their sleep by the blast. The explosion was heard even three thousand miles away on Rodriguez Island, where people mistook it for cannon fire.

Although no one lived on Krakatoa, the eruption caused thousands of deaths. The explosion set off huge waves—some as tall as five-story buildings. They traveled at over three hundred miles per hour. These waves killed people and destroyed villages on the nearby islands of Java and Sumatra. About 37,000 people were drowned.

After the eruption, people in many parts of the world found volcanic ash and dust in their streets and backyards. But much of the volcanic matter was blown so high into the atmosphere that it circled the earth several times before it landed. This matter—dust and acid droplets—produced colorful atmospheric effects for two years. The sun sometimes looked blue or green through the volcanic matter. The moon sometimes appeared to have a blue halo.

The same volcanic forces that had created Krakatoa had destroyed it—almost. A small part of the island was left standing. At first it was completely lifeless. But four months after the blast, scientists found a spider on the island. They believed that it had been blown there by the wind. During the next few years, birds dropped seeds on the island and plants began to grow. Animals from nearby islands swam across the straits and began to populate the island.

In 1925, a new volcanic island raised its head out of the sea very near Krakatoa. It was named *Anak Krakatoa,* meaning *Child of Krakatoa.* The child of Krakatoa is still growing from

The volcanic island called Anak Krakatoa was born in 1925 (above).

volcanic activity. Everyone hopes that when it grows up the child of Krakatoa won't be as bad as its parent.

Tomboro-The Volcano that Changed the Weather

The island of Sumbawa is located about nine hundred miles east of Krakatoa. There is a volcano named Mount Tomboro on this island. Mount Tomboro was thought to be dead until 1815. That year it erupted and caused great loss of life. Ash, wind, and waves killed about twelve thousand people. More than fifty thousand others died from hunger due to the destruction of crops.

The 1815 Tomboro blast apparently caused a worldwide change in weather. The year 1816 was very cold. In the United

States, the state of Vermont had a foot of snow in June, and it snowed there in July and August. Pennsylvania had frosts every month of the year. Around the world, the cold weather killed crops and livestock. People called 1816 the "Year Without a Summer."

How could a volcanic eruption create such a big change in weather? Tomboro sent about 150 million metric tons of volcanic dust high up into the atmosphere. Some of the sun's heat was blocked by this dust.

Some scientists believe that the Ice Age was brought about by volcanoes. They feel that times of great volcanic activity lowered temperatures enough to cause long periods of cold. There is some evidence to support this theory. Studies of rocks show that there *was* more volcanic activity during the Ice Age than at other times.

Santorini - The Volcano that Ended a Civilization

About five thousand years ago, the first important civilization in the Mediterranean area was established. This was the Minoan civilization. It flourished on the island of Crete and on other islands near Greece.

The Minoans built large palaces and lovely homes. Their artists created pottery, vases, and jewelry. The Minoans had their own system of writing as well as a number system. Minoan merchants sent out ships loaded with products to Egypt and other ports on the Mediterranean Sea.

Then, in about the year 1400 B.C., the Minoan culture suddenly ended. For many years it was thought that invaders had conquered the Minoans. Then in the late 1800s, miners struck a large layer of volcanic ash on the island of Santorini, near Crete. Ruins of houses and human bones were found beneath the ash. In 1956, a scientist named Dr. Angelos Galanapoulos used a method called *carbon-14 dating* to determine the age of the ash-covered houses and bones. According to the tests, they dated back to the year 1400 B.C. The conclusion was that a volcano on Santorini had exploded at about this time and produced the ash.

Scientists figured out the events that ended the Minoan culture. In about 1400 B.C., earthquakes caused death and destruction in Minoan cities. Then the volcano on Santorini erupted. Much of Santorini was blown up and sank into the sea. This eruption produced huge waves, which destroyed Minoan towns on the coasts of Crete and other islands.

Few bodies have been found in the eruption area. Before the eruption, many Minoans may have sailed off to Greece, where they helped build the great Greek civilization.

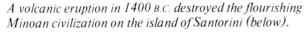

A volcanic eruption in 1400 B.C. destroyed the flourishing Minoan civilization on the island of Santorini (below).

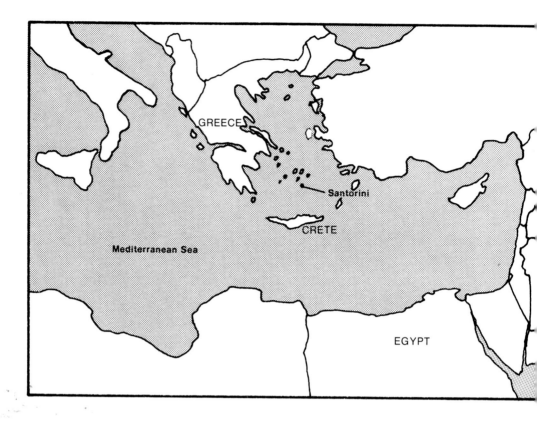

There are other interesting aspects to the Santorini eruption. For thousands of years, stories have been told about a lost island named "Atlantis." That island is said to have sunk beneath the sea. When Santorini blew up, much of *it* sank beneath the sea. Atlantis may really have been the volcanic island of Santorini.

There even may be a reference to Santorini in the Bible. In Exodus, you can read about Moses leading the Jewish people out of Egypt. This is thought to have occurred at about the time of the Santorini eruption. The Bible states that before Moses led his people from Egypt:

> . . . there was a thick darkness in all the land of Egypt three days: They saw not one another. . .

Ancient Egyptian writing also mentions a period of darkness that occurred at about this time. Some scholars think that the darkness referred to in both the Bible and the Egyptian writing was caused by ash from Santorini.

Of course, studying an eruption that occurred 3,400 years ago is difficult. Scientists cannot be absolutely certain about everything that happened. But they are still digging on Santorini to learn more about this eruption.

The Hawaiian Islands - The State that Was Built by Volcanoes

Millions of years ago, cracks opened on the floor of the Pacific Ocean. Lava came out of these cracks and piled up on the ocean floor. The lava formed underwater mountains. These mountains grew taller as more volcanic eruptions occurred beneath the sea. Eventually, the mountains raised their heads above the water. These volcanic mountaintops are the Hawaiian Islands.

Evidence of past volcanic activity can be seen in many places in the Hawaiian Islands. There is a black sand beach on the island of Hawaii (the Big Island). This sand is made of lava grains. Volcanic mountains also can be seen on the islands.

Heart-shaped Lake Waiau (below) is located on the slopes of Mauna Kea, one of Hawaii's many volcanic mountains.

Lava erupted from Hawaiian
volcanoes continues to add
land to the islands. The
pictures on this page and
the bottom of page 47 show
lava flows from a 1973
eruption of Mauna Ulu Crater
on the slopes of Kilauea
Volcano.
The center picture on
page 47 shows a dramatic
"lava waterfall." During
a 1973 eruption of the
double-pitted Pauahi Crater
on Kilauea, lava flowed from
one pit of the crater down
into the other.
Evidence of past volcanic
activity can be seen in many
places on the Hawaiian
Islands. The picture at the
top of page 47 shows lava
rock formations at Keanae,
on the island of Maui.

*In 1942, army bombers blasted the rivers of lava from
Mauna Loa (above) to divert the lava from the city of Hilo.*

Some of Hawaii's volcanoes are still active. On the island of
Hawaii stands the biggest volcanic mountain in the world—
Mauna Loa. When Mauna Loa erupts, it produces large
amounts of lava. In 1926, lava from Mauna Loa swept away
an entire fishing village. In 1933, and again in 1942, it was
feared that a lava flow from Mauna Loa would destroy the city
of Hilo. Both times, the United States Army sent up planes
that bombed the lava and changed its course.

Kilauea, another volcano on Hawaii Island, is nicknamed
the "drive-in volcano." People drive close to it to watch the
bubbling lava. Near Kilauea, a crater called Kilauea Iki sent
lava almost two thousand feet up into the air in 1959. In this

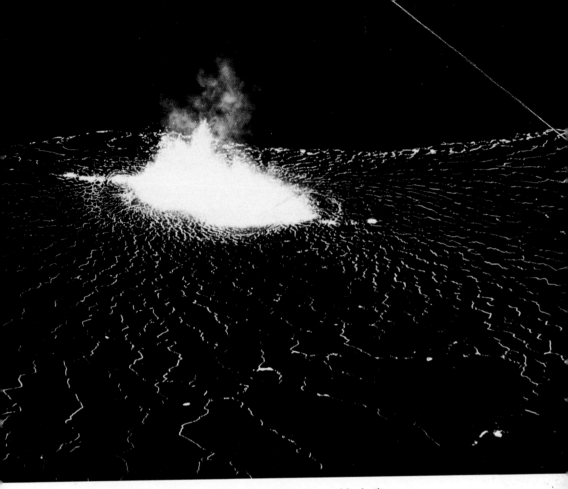

*This night photo shows the intricate pattern formed by boiling
lava from a 1952 eruption of the Halemaumau Volcano in Hawaii.*

1959 eruption, the temperature of the lava was measured at
2,100° F.

Compared to other volcanoes, those on Hawaii have mild
eruptions. They are known for their lava flows rather than for
great bursts of ash and gas. Lava usually flows slower than
five miles per hour—slow enough to allow people to get away.
This fact makes it possible for scientists at the Hawaiian
Volcano Observatory to study the Hawaiian volcanoes at very
close range.

Hawaii's volcanoes also erupt at frequent intervals. Every
time a volcano erupts in Hawaii, more land is created and the
the state grows a little bit bigger.

Parícutin-A Volcano Born in Modern Times

Only rarely are human beings able to witness the birth of a volcano. But in 1943, in the village of Parícutin, Mexico, people watched as a brand-new volcano was born.

A farmer named Dionisio Pulido lived in Parícutin. For years, Dionisio had known about a strange hole in his cornfield. When he stood near this small hole he heard sounds coming from underground. Also, the ground around the hole felt warm. Dionisio thought this hole was very strange, but it had been there for many years without causing any problem.

In early 1943, Dionisio noticed smoke coming out of the hole. The ground in his field felt even warmer than usual. There were also earthquakes in the village of Parícutin. They were getting stronger and stronger each day. Nevertheless, Dionisio had plowing to do. On February 20, 1943, he was out in his field with his wife and a friend. Suddenly there was a big earthquake. Smoke shot up out of the hole, and then out came ashes and stones.

Dionisio, his wife, and the friend left the field. Rock and ash built up around the hole very rapidly. When Dionisio came back to his field the next day, he found thirty feet of material piled up around the hole. The hole in Dionisio's cornfield was a volcano. And the mountain of material that was piling up around the hole was a volcanic mountain.

Scientists heard about the newborn volcano, and they came to watch it grow. In two days the volcano had created a 150-foot-high cinder cone. By the time the volcano was a week old, it had created a mountain more than 500 feet tall. Eventually, the volcanic mountain grew to be nearly 2,000 feet high. This new mountain was named Parícutin.

Parícutin Volcano (above) was born in 1943.

The mountain covered Dionisio's property. The whole village of Parícutin was destroyed by a layer of ash, as was the nearby city of San Juan. No one was killed, however, because the government of Mexico wisely moved the people out.

For the next nine years, Parícutin erupted lava, ash, and cinders. Then, in 1952, it went to sleep.

Left: The hills behind the harbor at Heimaey Island, Iceland are silhouetted against the blazing lava and ashes of a 1973 eruption of Helgafjell Volcano.
Below: A 1928 eruption of Mount Etna, in Sicily.

Above: Villarica Volcano in the Chilean Andes sends up steam.
Right: The crater of Taal Volcano in the Philippines shown during a 1968 eruption.

6/RINGS OF FIRE ON EARTH AND VOLCANOES ON OTHER WORLDS

You've read about a few of Earth's most famous volcanic mountains and eruptions. Here are short descriptions of some other volcanoes on our planet:

Aconcagua — At 22,834 feet above sea level, this volcano in Argentina is the highest peak in all the Western Hemisphere.

Mount Agung — An eruption of this volcano in Indonesia killed more than 1,500 people in 1963.

Cotopaxi — This beautiful volcano in Ecuador has erupted more than twenty-five times in the past four centuries.

Mount Etna — This famous volcano in Sicily has a long eruption history; an eruption and earthquake in 1669 claimed about 20,000 lives.

Mount Fuji — Every summer, thousands of Japanese people make a pilgrimage to the top of this volcano, which they consider sacred.

Hekla — Known as *The Back Gate to Hell,* this Icelandic volcano has erupted about fifteen times since 1104 A.D.

Mount Hood — This Cascade Range volcano in Oregon, U.S.A. has glaciers on its sides.

Ixtacihuatl — The name of this Mexican volcano means *white woman;* its three snow-clad peaks are shaped like the body of a sleeping woman.

Kilimanjaro — This volcano in Tanzania is the highest point in the continent of Africa.

Mayon — During the 1800s, this volcano in the Philippines erupted twenty-six times; some call it the loveliest-shaped volcano in the world.

Mont Pelée — A 1902 eruption of this Martinique volcano killed 38,000 people in the city of Saint-Pierre; only two persons in Saint-Pierre survived.

Mount Rainier — The Indians called this beautiful volcano in Washington, U.S.A. the *Mountain that was God.*

Mount Shasta — This Cascade Range volcano in California, U.S.A. was formed from lava flows.

Stromboli — This extremely active volcano in the Mediterranean Sea is called *The Lighthouse of the Mediterranean* because sailors have long steered their ships by its glow.

Surtsey — This volcanic island near Iceland rose out of the sea in 1963.

Taal — A 1911 eruption of this volcano in the Philippines cost 1,335 lives.

In all, there are thousands of inactive volcanoes on our planet. There are about five hundred active ones we know about on land. More active volcanoes lie under the ocean.

If you study a map of the earth's volcanoes, you will notice that they occur in patterns. Some regions have many volcanoes. Others have none. The most significant volcanic region on earth forms a ring-shaped pattern surrounding the Pacific Ocean. Scientists call this chain of volcanoes the *Ring of Fire.* There are more than three hundred active volcanoes

bove left: This diorama shows various kinds of volcanic activity, including a molten lava flow and e ejection of ash and steam. Above right: This aerial view of the continuing volcanic activity in Surtsey was taken in 1966, three years after the birth of the island. The map below shows the ain of volcanoes called the Pacific "Ring of Fire," the most significant volcanic region on earth.

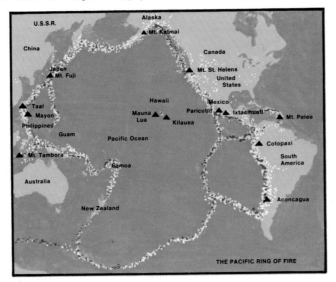

Heimaey Islanders, afraid that lava from the 1973 eruption of Helgafjell Volcano would choke their harbor, used hoses to deflect the flow. Below left: Where the lava stopped. Below right: Though the harbor was saved, many homes were lost to lava and smoking ash.

in the Pacific Ring of Fire. Other volcanic regions form ring-shaped patterns, too.

Why do volcanoes occur in these certain areas? In the 1960s, scientists developed the Plate Tectonic Theory, which they think explains it.

According to this theory, the earth's outer 60-mile shell is made up of a number of separate *plates*. There are seven big plates on our planet, and a number of smaller ones.

These plates are always moving about a bit—perhaps an inch a year. As they move, they carry land with them. In some places, moving plates overlap and rub against each other. This rubbing creates great heat. One plate starts to melt and the melted rock rises as magma, eventually forming volcanoes.

In other places, plates spread away from each other. This opens a space for magma to make its way up to the surface.

Either way, volcanoes are formed in the areas where two plates meet. The Pacific Ring of Fire, for example, occurs where the Pacific Plate meets other plates.

Volcanoes aren't the only upheavals that occur at plate boundaries. As the plates move, they break underground rock, causing earthquakes.

Hot Spots

Volcanoes sometimes occur in the middle as well as at the edges of plates. In some places—no one yet knows why—there are "hot spots" beneath the plates. These are places where the temperature is thought to be hotter than normal. At these hot spots, magma from the mantle makes its way up through the middle of a plate. The magma bursts out through the crust, forming a volcano.

Over many years, different areas of the slowly moving plate go over the hot spot. In this way, one hot spot can produce a whole chain of volcanoes. The Hawaiian Islands are volcanic mountains that were created by a hot spot. When you look at a map of the Hawaiian Islands, you can see the path that the plate made as it moved over the hot spot.

Volcanoes on Other Worlds

Volcanoes are not limited to Earth. During the 1970s, astronauts brought back volcanic rocks from the moon. The moon has flat areas, called *maria*. They were formed long ago when seas of lava flooded the moon's surface and then hardened. Narrow valleys, called *rilles,* also may have been created by lava flows. Many of the moon's craters were formed by meteorites. But astronomers think that some of them may have been created by volcanoes. It appears that the moon's main volcanic activity occurred long ago, and that there is little of it there today.

The planets, too, show evidence of volcanic activity. The smallest planet, Mercury, appears to have had some lava flows. The red planet, Mars, has many volcanoes. The largest volcano yet discovered in our solar system is on Mars. Its name is Olympus Mons, and it is about three times the size of Earth's biggest volcano—Mauna Loa. Venus, the closest planet to Earth, also has very large volcanoes.

In the late 1970s, the United States sent spacecraft to study Jupiter. The spacecraft took pictures of eruptions occurring on Io, one of Jupiter's many moons.

Future space explorations will give us more knowledge about volcanic activity on far-off worlds.

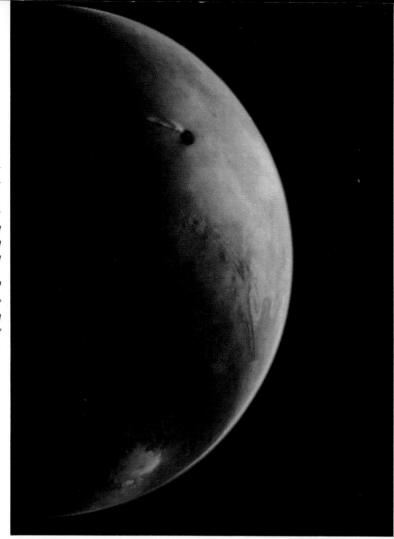

Right: This photo taken by Viking Orbiter 2 shows Ascreaus Mons, one of the giant Martian volcanoes, with cloud plumes on its western flank. Below: A Voyager 2 photo of two blue volcanic eruption plumes on Io, one of Jupiter's moons.

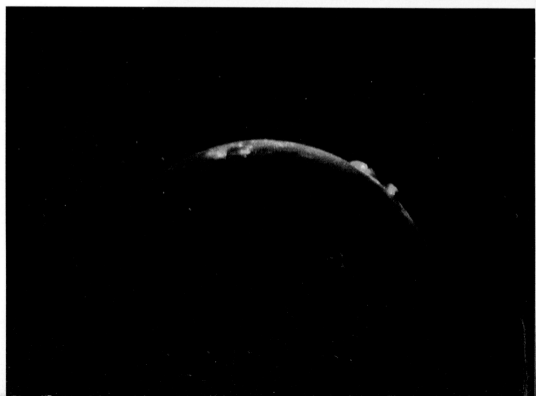

7/GIFTS FROM VOLCANOES

Death and destruction are the immediate effects of volcanoes. But, over long periods of time, volcanoes have many positive aspects.

The Formation of Land

Land is one of volcanoes' greatest gifts. The Hawaiian Islands and Iceland were formed by volcanoes. Even now, volcanoes beneath the seas are in the slow process of forming new lands.

This volcano was photographed as it erupted from the depths of the Pacific Ocean off Japan to create a new volcanic island.

Fertile Soil

Immediately after an eruption, volcanic ash can destroy crops. Over many years, however, volcanic ash and lava place minerals in the soil. These minerals enrich the soil and make it excellent for growing crops.

Uses of Volcanic Rocks

People have always found uses for the rocks thrown out by volcanoes. Obsidian is a kind of glass that forms when some lava cools. Because obsidian can be broken into sharp-edged splinters, early people used it to make spearheads, knives, and arrowheads.

Pumice is another kind of rock formed by quickly cooling lava. Because pumice contains many bubbles, it is very light. Dentists use pumice to clean teeth. Ground-up pumice is also used in making a kind of soap.

Valuable Minerals

Diamonds—the hardest substance on earth—are also one of the most valuable. Most diamonds have been found deep underground, in what are called *pipes*. Pipes are the necks of extinct volcanoes. It is thought that the pressure and heat of past volcanic eruptions created diamonds from carbon.

Volcanic eruptions also have brought many valuable minerals up near the earth's surface, where they can be mined. Gold, silver, and copper are just three of the valuable metals found in volcanic regions.

Heat and Electricity

In many places magma creates pools of water known as hot springs. In Iceland, most of the homes are heated by water from volcanic hot springs.

In California, Italy, and New Zealand, volcanic steam is used to generate electricity.

If hot springs and volcanic steam can produce heat and electricity, just think how much energy could be harnessed from volcanic eruptions. Scientists say that the 1952 eruption of Kilauea could have provided almost half the energy needed by the United States during the eruption period. Some geologists think that volcanic eruptions could provide *all* the energy needed by the world. Some of them are trying to find ways of harnessing that energy.

The Beauty and Intrigue of Volcanoes

Part of the attraction of volcanic mountains is their beauty. But even during times of deadly eruption, volcanoes have always intrigued human beings. Some people charter airplanes for flights over active volcanoes. Others try to get close to volcanoes while officials are working to keep people away. Even those of us who prefer to keep a safe distance from volcanoes find it fascinating to learn about them from books, newspapers, and television.

Why do people find volcanoes so intriguing? Perhaps the excitement comes from seeing something so unusual. Possibly the intrigue lies in a volcano's great physical power. Or perhaps volcanoes help us realize that our changing planet is not always a peaceful, safe place.

Glossary

Active volcano   One that has erupted or has shown signs of erupting within the past few years

Ash, volcanic   Hot rock fragments less than a fifth of an inch in diameter that explode from a volcano

Bomb, volcanic   The biggest rocks blown out of a volcano; some weigh many tons

Cinder cone volcano   A cone-shaped mountain built from eruptions of cinders, ash, and other rock fragments

Composite volcano   A mountain shaped like an upside-down *V* that is made up of lava and rock fragments

Core   The very center of the earth

Crust   The outside layer of the earth

Dormant volcano   One that is currently inactive but that has erupted within the past several centuries

Dust, volcanic   The smallest hot rock fragments that explode from a volcano

Earthquake   A shaking of the earth believed to be caused by movement of the earth's plates against or away from one another

Eruption, volcanic   The violent release of lava, gas, ash, or rock from a volcano

Extinct volcano   One that is inactive and not expected to become active again

Gas, volcanic   Gas released from lava during a volcanic eruption

Gas detector   An instrument that detects unusual gases escaping from under the ground

Geologist   A scientist who studies the earth

Hot spot   A place beneath one of the earth's plates where the temperature is hotter than normal, making it possible for magma to burst through the crust and form a volcano

Hot spring   A pool of water heated by magma

Landslide   The rapid slide of earth down a mountain, often caused by a volcanic eruption or an earthquake

Lava   Molten rock, or magma, that pours out of a volcano onto the surface of the earth

Magma   Molten rock beneath the surface of the earth

Magma chamber   A huge underground reservoir of magma, or molten rock

Mantle   The layer of the earth below the crust and above the core

Mudflow   A mass of mud that flows downhill

Observatory, volcano   A place from which scientists study volcanoes

Obsidian   A type of glass that forms when some lava cools

Plate Tectonic Theory   A scientific belief that the earth's crust is made up of a number of rigid, slowly moving plates

Pumice   A light, volcanic rock containing many holes

Pacific Ring of Fire   A ring-shaped chain of volcanoes encircling the Pacific Ocean

Seismograph   An instrument that detects earthquakes

Shield volcano   A mountain with gentle slopes formed almost completely by lava flows

Thermometer   An instrument that measures temperature

Tiltmeter   An instrument that measures swelling of the earth

Volcano   The opening in the earth's crust through which magma erupts, or the mountain formed by material erupted from the opening

Volcanologist   A scientist who studies volcanoes

Volcanology   The study of volcanoes

Photo Credits

R. HOBLITT, UNITED STATES GEOLOGICAL
  SURVEY (USGS)—Cover
J. ROSENBAUM, USGS—Page 2
ROGER WERTH—Pages 4, 19
D.R. MULLINEAUX, USGS—Page 6
C. DAN MILLER, USGS—Page 7 (top left and right)
P.W. LIPMAN, USGS—Page 7 (bottom)
UPI—Pages 8, 9, 12, 29, 36, 38, 45, 48, 49, 52, 59
D. MAY, USGS—Page 10 (top)
D. McKNIGHT, USGS—Pages 10 (bottom), 11 (bottom)
© 1980 K. and D. STOFFEL—Pages 11 (top), 15, 16
R.L. SCHUSTER, USGS—Page 11 (middle)
K. SEGERSTROM, USGS—Pages 27, 51

J. VALLANCE, USGS—Page 30
HISTORICAL PICTURE SERVICE, INC.—
  Pages 34, 35, 37, 41
SANDRA CHRYSTYCZ—Page 43
J.C. RATTÉ, USGS—Pages 46, 47 (middle and bottom)
CHANDLER FORMAN—Pages 47 (top),
  55 (bottom left and right)
COURTESY, FIELD MUSEUM OF NATURAL
  HISTORY—Page 55 (top left)
JULES D. FRIEDMAN, USGS—Page 55 (top right)
NASA—Page 58
LEN MEENTS (ART)—Pages 24, 28, 44, 55
COVER PHOTOGRAPH—The ash plume from the
  July, 1980 eruption of Mount St. Helens drifts to the
  northeast as the sun sets.

About the author

Dennis Fradin attended Northwestern University on a partial creative writing scholarship and graduated in 1967. He has published stories and articles in such places as *Ingenue, The Saturday Evening Post, Scholastic, Chicago, Oui,* and *National Humane Review.* His previous books include the Young People's Stories of Our States series for Childrens Press and *Bad Luck Tony* for Prentice-Hall. He is married and the father of three children.

About the artist

Len Meents studied painting and drawing at Southern Illinois University and after graduation in 1969 he moved to Chicago. Mr. Meents works full time as a painter and illustrator. He and his wife and child currently make their home in LaGrange, Illinois.